*Twinkle Universe Presents*

# Perfect!
# A Day in the Life
# of Ricky Rabbit
*Type 1 or The Perfectionist in Us All*

**The Enneagram for Children Series**

***Kolleen Meyer-Krikac, M.S. Ed.
and Devan Martin***

***Illustrated by Karissa Bettendorf***

## In Dedication

To my husband, Quinn for all of your love and support and to my son, Kennedy for always teaching me more about myself and others. ~Kolleen (Mom)

To my Enneagram teachers Russ Hudson and Don Riso. To my loving husband Jeff Martin and my beloved father for his support from the other side! ~Devan

The illustrations in this book were created using watercolor and ink.

**Perfect! A Day in the Life of Ricky Rabbit**

Published by Kolleen Meyer-Krikac Publishing

4830 Wilshire Blvd., Suite 102

Lincoln, NE 68504

ISBN: 978-0-9992849-26

Library of Congress Control Number: 2021925102

Twinkle is always in the night sky, observing young ones with a watchful eye.

The Moon notices with her gaze on Earth when young ones are having a bad day.

"Twinkle, I need you to ride a moonbeam of love down to Earth so this young one can see himself in a new light."

5

"Ricky Rabbit couldn't go to sleep because he was thinking about his bad day."

Ricky Rabbit remembered seeing his friends in the swimming pool splashing and laughing. He told them, "Stop! Why are you making a mess?"

Ella Elephant said, "Come play with us! We are having fun!"

Ricky Rabbit replied, "That doesn't look like fun. That looks messy!" Mikey Monkey and Ella Elephant continued to splash and play.

Ricky Rabbit got frustrated and told his friends, "It's not okay to make a mess, even if you are playing. Why won't you listen to me? This is no fun! I'm going home!" He stomped away with his arms folded.

8

When Ricky Rabbit arrived at home, he walked into the kitchen and saw Mama Rabbit starting to make dinner.

"Welcome home, Ricky. I hope you had fun with your friends at the pool. You are really growing up, so I have a job for you. Would you like to learn how to cut carrots for the soup?" asked Mama Rabbit.

Ricky was afraid of making a mistake and replied, "Okay, but will you show me the right way?"

"Of course, I will teach you how to do it," said Mama Rabbit.

Ricky Rabbit worked very hard to make sure all of the carrots were sliced the same size like Mama Rabbit's but got frustrated and slammed down the knife when they weren't as perfect as hers.

"Ricky, what are you upset about?" Mama Rabbit asked.

Ricky Rabbit replied, "But Mama, it has to be perfect! I can't do it right!"

Mama Rabbit said, "Not for the soup, Honey Bunny. It doesn't have to be perfect. The soup will still taste delicious."

Ricky Rabbit had enough of cutting carrots so he went to the backyard where Dad Rabbit was planting carrots in the garden.

"Hi, Ricky. I'm glad you are here! I am planting the garden and could use your help. I will plant on this side. You start on that side and we will meet in the middle," Dad Rabbit said.

They worked very hard to plant all the carrots and stepped back to admire their work. Ricky Rabbit crossed his arms and stomped his feet.

"What's wrong, Ricky?" Dad Rabbit asked.

"Dad, the rows are supposed to be perfect. I messed it up and could do this better. Let me do it again!" said Ricky.

Dad said, "It's okay, Ricky. The carrots will grow, even if they aren't in a straight row."

After dinner, with his less than perfectly cut carrots in the soup, Ricky went to bed feeling frustrated about his day and remembered what went wrong.

Twinkle sees Ricky and whispers softly, "We are all made of the light of the stars. The light is inside you. Breathe out all of the bad feelings. You are loved, just as you are."

Twinkle sprinkles magic stardust as Ricky falls asleep. In his dreams, Ricky sees two paths. One path has a rainbow, butterflies, birds and pretty trees. It looks like fun. The other path has dead trees, sticker bushes, weeds and dark clouds. It doesn't look like fun.

Twinkle's light shines on the paths so Ricky can see and choose how he wants to feel.

16

Twinkle asks, "What if you let yourself have fun, too? How does soup taste even if carrots aren't cut perfectly? Even peas in a pod aren't all the same size. Can carrots grow even if they aren't in a straight row?"

Ricky wakes up in the morning, remembering his dream about the paths. He is seeing things in a new light. He decides to find his friends and see if they want to play. When he arrives at the pool, Ella Elephant and Mikey Monkey are playing and splashing.

Ricky begins to see that maybe it's okay to play and join in the fun, even if it is messy. Ricky thinks, "Maybe I can learn something from my friends who seem to have a lot more fun than I do. I will join them." Ricky jumps in the pool with a big splash.

After playing with his friends in the pool, Ricky goes home to tell Mama Rabbit about the fun he had. Mama Rabbit says, "I'm glad that you had a fun time with your friends. Would you like to help me cut the carrots again for the soup?"

Ricky thinks, "Maybe I can take some slow deep breaths and let the light in so I can see the good in me and in others."

He smiles as he cuts the carrots.

After helping Mama Rabbit cut the carrots, Ricky goes outside and looks at the garden. He sees the tufts of green carrot leaves coming up.

Ricky thinks, "It's okay to make mistakes because that is how I learn and grow. Dad seems perfectly happy with the way I did this."

Dad Rabbit gives him a fist bump and tells him "Good job!"

As Ricky goes to sleep with the Moon light and Twinkle light shining through his window, he remembers the wonderful day he had. He realizes his new way of thinking.

Ricky puts his hand on his heart, taking the Twinkle light in and thinks, "It's good to remember that I am Light. When I breathe, I remember the light inside me, just like the stars."

Some things take practice.
It's okay to make a mistake and learn.
It doesn't have to be perfect, but can be good enough.
I can have fun and play!
It's fun to learn
Make time to play
Be kind to yourself

Twinkle looks down on Ricky as he sleeps.

26

# Tips for Parents

**Words of encouragement for your Type 1/perfectionist child (or yourself)**

- Listen to what is worrying or bothering your child first.

- Let your child know it's okay to be frustrated.

- Acknowledge feelings such as frustration and anger as well as positive feelings. Emotions aren't good or bad. All feelings are part of life.

- Encourage your child to lighten up and laugh.

- Help your child to see the good in what's happening instead of looking for what's bad or wrong.

- Make sure your child isn't taking on too much responsibility.

# Activities

Encourage creativity. Plan creative play time without rules. Play with your child and show that you aren't doing it perfectly. Consider activities that allow your child to play without thinking about doing it right or having to do it better. Try these: riding a bike, playing in the yard, sidewalk chalk, swinging on swing set, swimming, blowing bubbles, picking wildflowers, going for a walk while talking about what you are seeing and hearing. Go to a park.

Give your child a reward while learning and making progress instead of looking for perfection. Focus on the process vs. the result. (Don't make a gold star or an A+ be the reward for perfection). Maybe celebrate for turning in the paper even before knowing the grade.

If your child is getting frustrated or angry, try questioning where he/she feels it in the body. Or if your child could get in the shape of the frustration, what would that shape be? Follow your child's lead and as best you can, get into the same shape as your child. Maybe have him/her choose a color for the emotion and color or scribble it.

Bedtime gratitude list. At bedtime, have your child share 3 things he/she is grateful for or appreciated about the day. Take 3 deep breaths. Then share things you are grateful for about each other. This helps children to be grateful for who they are instead of who they are not.

# "I am" statements

Recite "I am" statements out loud to help your child see himself/herself as they really are. Act like a reflection for them. Pick the 3 that fit best for your child and say them with your child in the morning and at night.

"I am strong." "I am healthy." "I am curious." "I am fun." "I am confident." "I am smart." "I am loved just as I am."

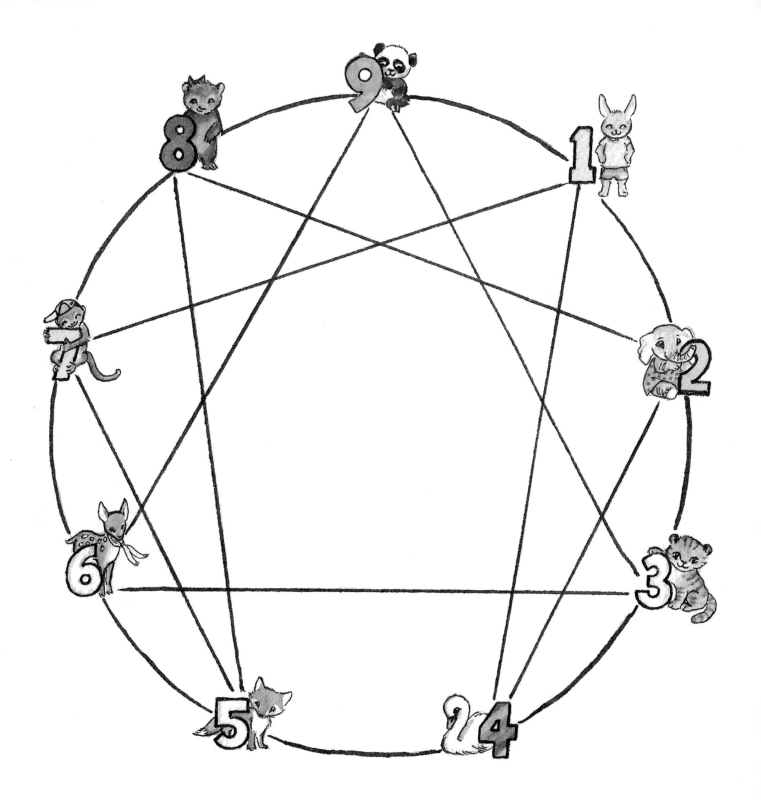

## About the Authors

Kolleen Meyer-Krikac, M.S. ED. is a former teacher and school counselor who has been in private practice as a professional counselor and life coach for the past 23 years. She is the author of How to Create Your Balanced Life and teaches classes for other counselors as well as individuals.

Devan Martin is a certified Life Coach, Hypnotist and teacher of the Enneagram. She has used her background from the last 20 years studying the Enneagram to help her clients in Personal Development.

Kolleen and Devan teach workshops and webinars about the Enneagram and decided that it would be a good idea to teach this subject to children and parents, too. They are excited to write a series of nine books to cover each of the personality types on the Enneagram so that parents and children have a greater understanding of themselves and how to deal with the challenges of each type.

Karissa Bettendorf is owner and artist at Karis Fine Arts. She lives in Lincoln Nebraska with her husband, son, and springer spaniel. When she is not painting, she loves to garden, bake, and read any book she can get her hands on!

## Added Note

The authors are donating 10% of the profits to St. Jude's Children's Hospital. Why St. Jude's? Since Devan has been donating to St. Jude's in recent years, she suggested that we donate to their cause due to their powerful message of hope to children and families. Kolleen's sister died of leukemia at the age of 14 and St. Jude's was there for her family. The fact that Karissa's son is named Jude also seemed to be a sign that this was the right choice for a charity we support.

Made in the USA
Middletown, DE
19 April 2022

64469236R00020